Hazel Moring —

April 1919 —

MARY MAGDALENE

THE WORKS OF MAURICE MAETERLINCK

ESSAYS

The Treasure of the Humble
Wisdom and Destiny
The Life of the Bee
The Buried Temple
The Double Garden
The Measure of the Hours
On Emerson, and Other Essays
Our Eternity
The Unknown Guest
The Wrack of the Storm

PLAYS

Sister Beatrice, and Ardiane and Barbe Bleue
Joyzelle, and Monna Vanna
The Blue Bird, A Fairy Play
Mary Magdalene
Péllèas and Mélisande, and Other Plays
Princess Maleine
The Intruder, and Other Plays
Aglavaine and Selysette

HOLIDAY EDITIONS

Our Friend the Dog
The Swarm
The Intelligence of the Flowers
Death
Thoughts from Maeterlinck
The Blue Bird
The Life of the Bee
News of Spring and Other Nature Studies
Poems

Mary Magdalene

A Play in Three Acts

BY
MAURICE MAETERLINCK

Translated by
ALEXANDER TEIXEIRA DE MATTOS

NEW YORK
DODD, MEAD AND COMPANY
1917

AUTHOR'S NOTE

I have borrowed from Mr. Paul Heyse's drama, *Maria von Magdala,* the idea of two situations in my play, namely, at the end of the first act, the intervention of Christ, who stops the crowd raging against Mary Magdalene with these words, spoken behind the scenes: "He that is without sin among you, let him cast the first stone;" and, in the third, the dilemma in which the great sinner finds herself, of saving or destroying the Son of God, according as she consents or refuses to give herself to a Roman.

Before setting to work, I asked the venerable German poet, whom I hold in the highest esteem, for his permission to develop those two situations, which, so to speak, were merely sketched in his play, with its incomparably richer plot than mine; and I offered to recognize his rights in whatever manner he thought proper. My respectful request was answered with a refusal, none too courteous, I regret to say, and almost threatening.

From that moment, I was bound to consider that the words from the Gospel, quoted above, are common property; and that the dilemma of which I speak is one of those which occur pretty frequently in dramatic literature. It seemed to me the more lawful to make use of it inasmuch as I had happened to imagine it in the fourth act of *Joyzelle,* in the same year in which *Maria von Magdala* was published and before I was able to become acquainted with that play.

I will add that, excepting the principle of these two situations, in all that concerns the subject of the play, the conduct of the action, the persons, the characters, the evolution and the atmosphere, our two works have absolutely nothing in common: not a phrase, not a cue of the one will be found in the other.

Having said this, I am happy to express to the aged master my gratitude for an intellectual benefit which is none the less great for being involuntary.

MAURICE MAETERLINCK.

ACT I

ACT I

(*The gardens of* Annœus Silanus *at Bethany. A Roman terrace. A quincunx. Marble benches, porticoes, statues. In the centre, a basin with a fountain. Arbours. Orange-trees and laurel-trees in stone vases. A balustrade on the right and left, overlooking the valley. A balustrade at the back, open at the middle to give access to a walk lined with plane-trees and statues and ending in a thick hedge of laurels which closes the garden.*)

SCENE I

(Enter Annœus Silanus *and* Lucius Verus)

Silanus

Here is the terrace, the glory of my little

domain: it reminds me of my terrace at Præneste, which was the crown of my desires. Here are my orange-trees, my cypresses and my oleanders. Here is the fishpond, the portico with the images of the gods: one of them is a statue of Minerva, discovered at Antioch. (*Pointing to the landscape on the left.*) And here you have the incomparable view over the valley, where spring already reigns. We hang midway in space. Admire the anemones streaming down the slopes of Bethany. It is as though the earth were ablaze beneath the olive-trees. Here I relish in peace the advantages of old age, which knows how to take pleasure in the past; for youth narrows the enjoyment of good things, by considering only those which are present. . . .

VERUS

At last! Here are trees and water and grass! . . . I had lost the memory of them since my arrival in this stony desert which men call Judæa. . . . But how comes it, O my good master, that you have taken up your abode near that dull and barren city, where the soil is abominable, where the men are ugly, churlish, crafty and mischievous, unclean and barbarous?

SILANUS

As you know, I came with the Procurator Valerius Gratus to Cæsarea; then I returned to Rome, where you were for some time my faithful and favourite pupil. But soon I became ashamed of teaching a wisdom whose certainties became more doubtful to my mind as the assurance wherewith I proclaimed them increased. I was brought back here, to this barbarous Judæa, by the strangest curiosity. During my first sojourn, I had begun to study the sacred books of the Jews. They are crude and bloodthirsty; but they also contain beautiful myths and the early efforts of an uncivilized but, at times, singular wisdom. They have not yet wearied me.

VERUS

Yes, our friend Appius, whom I met at Antioch, told me of your studies and of your sudden and inordinate passion for old Jewish books. . . .

SILANUS

He will be here shortly. . . .

VERUS

Who? Appius? . . . Is he at Jerusalem?

SILANUS

Did you not know? . . . But how long have you yourself been in this country? . . . In your letter of two days since, you did not tell me. . . .

VERUS

Nearly a week; and I wished to give my first leisure to you. I left Antioch to go to Jerusalem with the Procurator Pontius Pilate. He fears disturbances and will probably need the help of my old legionaries. . . .

SILANUS

The spacious, ample Appius, whose words are as rambling as his habits and bring together the most distant friends, spoke to me of you, even as he spoke to you of me. He told me that, when he had the good fortune to meet you at Antioch, you seemed a prey to some great unhappy love. . . .

VERUS

Which was that?

SILANUS

What! Can the handsomest of military tribunes, in his magnificent array, know more than one love that is not happy? . . . It concerned a woman of these regions, a Galilean, if I be not mistaken. . . .

VERUS

Mary of Magdala? . . . Did he speak to you of her? . . . Where is she? . . . I did not see her again; she left Antioch suddenly; and I lost trace of her. . . .

SILANUS

But why did she not listen to you? . . .

Appius declared to me that she sets the men of this country, it is true, at naught, but shows herself not at all inexorable to the Roman knights. . . .

VERUS

It is one of those riddles of womankind which our duties as soldiers hardly leave us time to solve. She did not appear to dislike me; at least, the dislike which she affected was not without a harsh gentleness. . . . But there was mingled with it a certain incomprehensible dread, which made her timidly avoid me. . . . Besides, she seemed lately to have suffered a great sorrow, for which she has already, I hear, consoled herself more than once. . . .

SILANUS

I do not know; and all this does not seem to me so very discouraging. After all, why afflict one's self with what the gods created for pleasure? . . . Appius, therefore, wished me to cure you, by my wise counsels, of an ill that saddens you needlessly. But, first, do you love her as much as Appius declares? His talk is often extravagant and heedless. . . .

VERUS

I desired her, I still desire her, as I have never desired any woman. . . .

SILANUS

You speak wisely in not separating, from the outset, desire and love. Besides, I understand. She is certainly the loveliest of all the many women whom I have admired in my life.

VERUS

What! . . . You have seen her? . . . Is she at Jerusalem then?

SILANUS

She is even nearer to us than Jerusalem, which is fifteen stadia from Bethany. . . . (*Drawing him a little to the right*). Come to this portico and look over there, at the bottom of the valley. . . . What do you see? . . .

VERUS

I see olive-trees, paths, tombs. . . . Then I see the pediments of palaces or temples, columns, cypresses. . . . One might think one's self in the outskirts of Rome. . . . But I do not perceive. . . .

SILANUS

It was Herod the Great, a sort of raving lunatic, but given to building, who filled this valley with splendid palaces more Roman than those of Rome herself.

. . . But look half-way down the hill, to the left of those three tall cypresses, three or four stadia from here. . . . Do you espy one of the most beautiful marble villas? . . .

VERUS

The villa with the wide white steps leading to a semicircular colonnade adorned with statues? . . .

SILANUS

That is where she has retired. . . .

VERUS

Mary Magdalene? . . . In that solitude, so far from the city? . . .

SILANUS

She told me that she was fleeing from the fanaticism of the Jews, the tumult and the sickening smells, which increase twofold at Jerusalem as the Passover approaches. . . .

VERUS

Then you see her? . . . You have spoken to her? . . .

SILANUS

The good Appius, knowing that the sight of a young and beautiful woman delights my eyes without endangering them, did not dissuade her from coming up to the house of a disarmed and harmless old man. . . .

VERUS

What did she say to you? . . . What impression did she make upon you? . . .

SILANUS

She was clad in a raiment that seemed woven of pearls and dew, in a cloak of

Tyrian purple with sapphire ornaments, and decked with jewels that rendered a little heavier this eastern pomp. As for her hair, surely, unloosed, it would cover the surface of that porphyry vase with an impenetrable veil of gold. . . . .

VERUS

I speak of her intelligence, her character. . . . Do not mistake: she is no vulgar courtezan. . . . She has other attractions, binding love more firmly. . . .

SILANUS

I minded only her beauty, which is real and contents the eye. . . . However, we can judge better presently: she will soon be coming. . . .

VERUS

She is coming here? . . . But does

she know that she will find me with you? . . .

SILANUS

Most certainly. It seemed to me that this meeting would do more to assuage your malady than the wise counsels threatened by Appius. . . .

VERUS

But she? . . . What did she say when she learnt that. . . .

SILANUS

She smiled with a quivering and pensive grace. . . . The other guests will be our indispensable Appius and Cœlius, your fellow-pupil at Præneste. . . . I hope that they will bring our poor friend Longinus, who, three weeks ago, lost a little daughter two years old. . . . I will try to console him, by good and persuasive arguments, for a sorrow certainly disproportionate to his loss. We shall have, among other dishes—all excellent, I hope,—two fish from the Jordan, new to you, which, dressed by Davus, my old cook. . . . But I hear the sound of the double flute. . . . It must be the litter of the queen of Bethany and Jerusalem at the threshold of my house . . . Your eyes will soon behold the soft light which they have missed and mine the smile that pleases them. . . . unless the silver mirrors in the Atrium delay her longer than they should . . . .

VERUS

She is here. . . .

(ENTER, *on the right,* MARY MAGDALENE. *She is followed by some slaves, whom she dismisses with a harsh and imperious gesture.)*

SCENE II

THE SAME, MARY MAGDALENE

SILANUS (*going up to receive* MARY MAGDALENE

"Who is this that cometh out of the wilderness like pillars of smoke, perfumed with myrrh and frankincense? . . . Who is she that looketh forth as the morning, fair as the moon, clear as the sun and terrible as an army with banners," as your sacred books sing at the approach of the Shulamite? . . . .

MARY MAGDALENE

Do not speak to me of my sacred books. I loathe them, as I loathe everything that comes from that deceitful and sordid, greedy and mischievous nation. . . .

VERUS (*coming forward to greet her in his turn*)

I will say then, in the Roman fashion, "Hail to the eldest daughter of Aglaia, youngest and happiest of the Graces!"

MARY MAGDALENE

Pity me, instead of praising me. I was robbed, last night, of my Carthaginian rubies, besides twelve of my finest pearls; and, what I feel even more, my Babylonian peacock and all the murænæ in my fishpond. . . .

VERUS

Who dared commit such manifest sacrilege? . . .

MARY MAGDALENE

I do not know. . . . I have had the slaves in charge of the aviary and the fish-pond beaten with rods and put to the torture: they have confessed nothing and I believe that they know nothing. . . .

VERUS

Have you no clue, no suspicion?

SILANUS

The theft amazes me, for the country is safe. . . . I have been living here for nigh six years; and no one has ever tried to rob me of an atom of my wisdom, which is never under lock and key and is the only precious thing that I possess. . . . The Jew is crafty, sly and evil-minded; he practises cheating and usury as well as most of the cringing virtues and vices; but he nearly always avoids frank, straightforward theft, honest theft, if one may say so. . . .

MARY MAGDALENE

I at first suspected some Tyrian workmen who are fitting one of the rooms in my villa with those movable panels which are changed at every course, so that the walls may harmonize with the dishes covering the table. . . .

VERUS

I have seen some like them in the house of our Governor, Pomponius Flaccus, at Antioch; but I did not know that this fashion, so new to Rome herself, had already made its way into this remote country. . . .

MARY MAGDALENE

Nor will you find it, except in my house; and the last palace of the Tetrarch Antipas is still without it. . . . Therefore I began by suspecting those workmen; but I have proofs that they are innocent. I now feel sure that the thieves must be sought among that band of vagrants and prowlers who have been infesting the country for some time. . . .

SILANUS

The famous band of the Nazarene. . . .

MARY MAGDALENE

Even so. Their leader, I hear, is a sort of unwashed brigand who entices the crowds with a rude kind of sorcery and, on the pretence of preaching some new law or doctrine, lives by plunder and surrounds himself with fellows capable of everything. . . . Besides, I have other causes to complain of them. . . . Two days ago, when I was walking in my gardens, under the portico that divides them from the road, a dozen wretches, belonging to that band, insulted me foully and threatened me with stones. . . . It is becoming intolerable; and it is time that the countryside were rid of them. . . .

VERUS

I have heard about those people. . . . I know that the authorities have their eyes upon them. . . . I will have them watched more closely. For that matter, if you wish, it would be easy for me to arrest their leader. . . .

MARY MAGDALENE

Do so, I pray you, and as soon as possible. . . . I should be especially grateful to you. . . .

SILANUS

I believe that you are misled. The robbers, in my opinion, must not be looked for there. I am in a fairly good position to know the band, seeing that, for five or six days, it has been gathered near my house. I have even had the pleasure—for everything turns to pleasure at my age—I have even had the pleasure of attending one of their meetings. It was near the old road to Jericho. The leader was speaking in the midst of a crowd covered with dust and rags, among whom I observed a large number of rather repulsive cripples and sick. They seem extremely ignorant and exalted. They are poor and dirty, but I believe them to be harmless and incapable of stealing more than a cup of water or an ear of wheat. . . . They were listening greedily to a more or less silly anecdote, the story of a son who returns to his father after squandering his patrimony. . . . I did not hear the end, for they looked upon me with a certain suspicion. . . . But the Galilean, or the Nazarene, as they call him here, is rather curious; and his voice is of a penetrating and peculiar sweetness. . . . He appears to be the son of a carpenter. . . . I will tell you more of him, I know many interesting things about him; but permit me first to go to the other side of the house, which commands the road, to see if my belated guests are not in sight. . . .

(*He* GOES OUT *on the left.*)

SCENE III

MARY MAGDALENE, VERUS

VERUS

I was not prepared for the joy of seeing you again, of your own consent, after your cruel words. They deprived me even of the hope that is sometimes left to those whom one would drive to despair. . . .

MARY MAGDALENE

I was stupid and foolish; but reason has returned; and I now know that the best love is not worth a tear. . . .

VERUS

Inasmuch as it is hardly the best, nor even a good love, as soon as it causes tears to be shed. . . .

MARY MAGDALENE

There is no more best or worst love for me. Until lately, I lived among falsehoods by which others profited; for the past six months, I have lived among truths by which I myself profit.

VERUS

What do you mean? . . . .

MARY MAGDALENE

That I sell myself more skilfully and dearer than before.

VERUS

Magdalene! . . . You slander yourself! . . .

MARY MAGDALENE

You would see, if your desire prompted you to try your fortune, that, on the contrary, I rate myself very highly.

VERUS

You will always rate yourself less highly than I do. You will not succeed in degrading yourself in my eyes; and I see in what you say no more than the just rebellion of a deeply wounded soul struggling against pain. . . .

MARY MAGDALENE

You are wrong: it is not a soul struggling, but one that is finding itself.

VERUS

I do not believe a word of it. However, I would rather spite or hatred gave you to me than lose you for the noblest of reasons; and, as it is a question only of rating you very highly, know, Magdalene, that from this moment you are mine. . . .

MARY MAGDALENE

May be. . . . But here is our host returning. We have nothing more to say to each other, for the moment. . . .

(ENTER, *on the left,* SILANUS, APPIUS *and* CŒLIUS.)

SCENE IV

THE SAME, SILANUS, APPIUS, CŒLIUS

APPIUS (*going to* MARY MAGDALENE)

"Venus has left Cyprus and soars above Jerusalem!" Or, rather, it is the fair Techmessa, who already brings back the smile to the lips of the son of Telamon! . . . Admire, O Cœlius, the magnificent image raised under this portico by Love and Beauty!

CŒLIUS

It is as though the azure sky were spread for them between those two columns.

SILANUS

The azure and the light seem happy only when environing youth and love. . . . But, to return to less dazzling images, better-suited to my head burdened with years, I observed that it must have been a sort of presentiment that urged us to speak, but a moment ago, of the Nazarene's band, for it was that same band which delayed our guests. . . .

APPIUS

Yes, imagine, when we approached the last cross-road down there, we found the whole country in a stir and the way blocked by a shouting, gesticulating throng, which was crowding round a blind man who saw! . . .

VERUS

Yes, that is one of those phenomena which one meets with nowhere except in Judæa. . . .

CŒLIUS

It was extraordinary! . . . The poor man, crushed against an old wall, rolled two drunk and virgin eyes, crying, "He is a prophet! He is a prophet! I see men as trees, walking!" And the crowd stamped all around for joy. He seemed dazed with the light. . . . .

APPIUS

Or rather with wine, for he was plainly staggering.

VERUS

And the Nazarene, did you see him? . . . .

APPIUS

No, he had just gone away, taking with him the most turbulent part of the crowd; but for that, we should never have been able to pass. . . .

MARY MAGDALENE

Yes, it appears that, when those ruffians crowd round their leader, they would not trouble to make way for Cæsar.

COELIUS

Where did he go? . . . I should be curious to see him. . . .

SILANUS

He cannot be very far. . . . Do you see that laurel-hedge, at the bottom of my garden? . . . It divides my little domain from the orchard of my neighbour, known as Simon the Leper. . . .

MARY MAGDALENE (*starting*)

What, your next neighbour is a leper? . . . You should have told us. . . .

SILANUS

Be reassured, lady, he has no leprosy now. . . .

APPIUS

I thought that one became a leper for life, just as one becomes a senator. . . .

This is another of the surprises of this monstrous Judæa. . . .

SILANUS

The Nazarene healed him.

CŒLIUS

Is he really healed? . . . As his next neighbour, you must know the truth. . . .

SILANUS

I know that he is as healthy in the face as the rose of Magdala and lily of Bethany whom you see before you; but I do not know if he was ever sick, not having seen him before his recovery. . . .

APPIUS

I thought so. . . . Besides, I have seen much more extraordinary magicians in Thrace and Egypt. . . . But, to return to this leper without leprosy, what happens behind that hedge and in the house of your mysterious neighbour?

SILANUS

The Nazarene has been his guest for the past three days. This Simon, his sister, his wife and, I believe, his brother-in-law are common people, who live on the produce of their olive-trees. They were timorous, peaceable neighbours; but, since the arrival of the Nazarene, everything is in commotion. It is a perpetual coming and going, a perpetual tumult. Their orchard is filled incessantly with a multitude of sick, of vagrants, of cripples, issuing from all the rocks in Judæa to beseech him whom, with loud cries, they call the Saviour of the World, the Son of David and King of the Jews. There are sometimes so many of them that they overflow into my garden. The hedge, as you see, has been trampled, crushed and even torn in certain places. Fortunately, the Nazarene's appearances are few and brief. Besides, this picturesque spectacle, despite its inconveniences, amuses and puzzles me.

(ENTER, *on the left, five or six* POOR FOLK.)

CŒLIUS

Who are those people?

SILANUS

What did I tell you? . . . . Here are half-a-dozen coming to ask for bread. . . .

APPIUS

Do they belong to this famous band?

MARY MAGDALENE

They are hateful and loathsome! . . . One of them has his face gnawed with an ulcer, another is almost naked, another is starving! . . .

APPIUS

They certainly lack shame, thus to flaunt ugliness and dread. . . .

SILANUS

Do not be uneasy: these will not long mar the pleasing grace of the porticoes that refresh our eyes. My gardener has discovered them; he is armed with a stout hoe and is driving them back uncivilly. . . . You see, they do not insist, they walk away in silence, hanging their heads. . . . And, now that we have occupied ourselves long enough with these unfortunate people, with their great leader and their maladies, let us think a little of ourselves and enjoy the delightful afternoon which spring-time sets before us. . . . My pleasure at seeing you here would be flawless, if only our old friend Longinus had yielded to Appius' entreaties and consented to accompany you. . . .

APPIUS

I never felt more keenly the vanity of the great eloquence which he himself taught me. To all my most convincing and well-stated arguments he replied with a sullen silence, or shook his head, repeating that he did not wish to throw a gloom over our happy party with his dismal presence. . . .

CŒLIUS

And yet it is quite three weeks since that child died. . . . I should not have thought that grief could have affected him so much. . . .

APPIUS

The more so as it concerned a child of

tender years, whom her father knew less well than did her nurse! . . .

SILANUS

There is something more astonishing yet, which clearly shows that the greatest wisdom is not so much to know as to conform to what one knows! . . . When, more than fifteen years ago, I lost a little boy who must have been of about the same age as the child whom he now mourns, Longinus undertook to console me. He wrote me an eloquent letter, wherein, relying on the authority of Metrodorus, Panætius and Hermachus, he proved that sorrow is not only useless, but ungrateful. I found and read the letter again this morning; and so striking are its more important passages that I know them almost by heart. . . . They were the loftiest words that human wisdom could utter against death and sorrow. . . . They protected me once. . . .

MARY MAGDALENE

What were the words? It is well to know anything that can relieve sorrow. . . .

SILANUS

"You expect consolation," he said; "you shall receive only reproaches. If you bear the death of a child with so little patience, what would you do if you had lost a friend? You ought to bring yourself to this frame of mind, that you were more pleased at having had him than grieved that you had him no longer. But most men reckon past advantages and pleasures as of no account. They bury friendship with their friend. . . ."

APPIUS

I recognize and hail the mighty wisdom of our venerable master.

SILANUS

Why does he not remember it, when misfortune strikes him? But why did I forget it myself, when I needed it most? . . . "I assure you," he added, "that of those whom we have loved, much remains to us after death has removed them. The time that is past is ours; and I see nothing of which we are more certain than of that which has been. The hope of the future makes us ungrateful for the benefits which we have received, as though the favours which we expect were not bound soon to be ranked among things past. Death has deprived you of a son so young that he could be of no promise to you yet; it is only a little time lost. There are instances without end of fathers losing infant children without shedding a single tear and returning to the senate after laying them in the grave. This is not unreasonable; for, in the first place, it is idle to give way to grief when grief can serve no purpose. And then it is unjust to complain of a misfortune that has befallen one person and still threatens all the others. Moreover, it is madness to complain, when there is so little distance between the one who is dead and the one who mourns him. Consider that all mankind, destined to one and the same end, is divided only by little intervals, even when they appear very great. He whom you think lost has only gone before. Since we must all travel the same road, is it not unworthy of a wise man to weep for one who has set out earlier than ourselves? To complain that the friend or the child is dead is to complain that he was ever born. We are all linked to the same fate. He who has come into the world must also leave it.

His stay may be longer, but the end is always alike. The time that elapses between the first day and the last is uncertain and variable. If you consider the wretchedness of life, it is long, even for a child; if you regard the duration, it is short, even for an old man."

MARY MAGDALENE

That would not have consoled me. . . . .

SILANUS

To console, lady, is not to do away with sorrow, but to teach one how to overcome it.

(*At this moment, there is heard rising from the roads, the paths and all the invisible country commanded by the terrace a noise, at first dull and confused, which gradually becomes more positive and precise. Sounds of a crowd forming and hurrying, stones rolling, children crying, dogs barking; shouts that grow more and more distinct: "This way! This way! . . . Come quickly! . . . Come down! . . . To the right, to the right! . . . He is there! . . . We saw him! . . . He is leaving the house! . . . To Simon's orchard! . . . Carry the palsied there! . . . Lead the blind! . . . Quick, quick, this way! . . . They say he is going to speak!" etc.)*

APPIUS

What is this? What is happening? . . .

VERUS

They are hurrying from every side! . . .

CŒLIUS

All the roads are covered with people running like madmen! . . . .

APPIUS

They seem to spring from the stones! . . . .

CŒLIUS

But what is happening? . . . They are disappearing behind those olive-trees. . . . .

VERUS

Here come two sick men carried on their beds. . . . .

CŒLIUS

A blind man falling! . . . .

APPIUS

What is the matter with them? . . . . Are they mad? . . .

VERUS

Who are those extraordinary creatures leaping among the rocks? . . . .

SILANUS

They are the men possessed by devils, coming out of the tombs. . . .

APPIUS

But, after all, what is happening? . . .

SILANUS

They have seen the Nazarene. . . .

MARY MAGDALENE

The Nazarene? . . . . Where is he? . . . .

SILANUS

He has probably just come out of Simon's house. They watch all his movements. As soon as he is seen, they bring the sick; and the fanatics come rushing up. . . . He must be walking in the neighbouring orchard. . . . (*Listening.*) Yes. . . . Do you hear the crowd humming like bees? . . . It is close to my laurel-hedge. . . .

APPIUS

Let us go and see. . . .

SILANUS

I do not advise you to. In the first place, those people are mostly very poor, extremely dirty and very unpleasant to come into touch with. . . . Then, you know the Jewish fanaticism. . . . In these moments of exaltation, the most inoffensive become dangerous; and the sight of the Roman toga and arms enrages them strangely. . . . Besides, we shall hear what happens quite well from where we stand. . . . Listen! . . . The cries are coming nearer still and increasing. . . .

(Behind the hedge that closes the end of the garden rise cries that sound nearer and nearer: "Hosannah! Hosannah! . . . Son of Man! . . . Lord, Lord, have pity! Lord, Son of David, heal the sick man! . . . . Master! Master! Lord! . . . Jesus of Nazareth, have pity on me! . . . Make way! . . . Silence, silence! . . . He is going to speak!" At these words, the tumult suddenly subsides. An incomparable silence, in which it seems as though the birds and the leaves of the trees and the very air that is breathed take part, falls with all its supernatural weight upon the countryside; and, in this silence, which weighs upon people on the terrace also, there rises, absolute sovereign of space

and the hour, a wonderful voice, soft and all-powerful, intoxicated with ardour, light and love, distant and yet near to every heart and present in every soul.)

THE VOICE

Blessed are the poor in spirit, for theirs is the kingdom of heaven! . . . Blessed are they that mourn, for they shall be comforted! . . . Blessed are the meek, for they shall inherit the earth! . . .

APPIUS

What is he saying? . . .

SILANUS

Listen! . . . It is rather curious. . . . .

THE VOICE

Blessed are they which do hunger and thirst after righteousness, for they shall be filled! . . . Blessed are the merciful, for they shall obtain mercy! . . .

MARY MAGDALENE

I want to see! . . . (*She rises and, as though irresistibly drawn by the divine voice, goes as if to descend the steps of the terrace and to make for the bottom of the garden.*)

SILANUS (*in a low voice, trying to hold her back*)

Do not go there! . . . .

THE VOICE

Blessed are the pure in heart, for they shall see God! . . .

MARY MAGDALENE

I will go! . . .

VERUS

I shall go with you. . . .

MARY MAGDALENE (*fiercely, imperiously*).

No! Nobody! . . . Let me be! . . . (*She goes down towards the hedge, as though fascinated.*)

THE VOICE

Blessed are the peacemakers, for they shall be called the children of God! . . . Blessed are they which are persecuted for righteousness' sake, for theirs is the kingdom of heaven! . . .

VERUS

Where is she going . . .

APPIUS

What is she doing? . . . She is mad! . . . She is trying to pass through the hedge! . . .

THE VOICE

Blessed are ye when men shall revile you and persecute you! . . . Rejoice and be exceeding glad, for great is your reward in heaven! . . .

VERUS

She has opened the gate of the garden! . . . She is in the orchard! . . .

SILANUS

Women sometimes have thoughts which wise men do not understand. . . .

VERUS

I shall go and join her; and, if I have to protect her against those . . .

SILANUS

Do no such thing. . . . They are listening to the voice and will not perceive her presence, whereas the sight and sound of your arms . . . Listen, listen to what he is saying: it is rather singular. . . . .

THE VOICE

But I say unto you, Love your enemies, bless them that curse you, do good to them that hate you and pray for them which despitefully use you! . . . .

(At that moment, cries, at first scattered, rise among the invisible crowd behind the hedge. A few words are distinguishable: "It is the Roman woman! The Roman woman! . . . The adulteress! . . . Shame! . . . Shame! Shame! . . . Magdalene! . . . The strumpet! . . . Drive her away, drive her away! . . ." Immediately afterwards, these cries are lost in a violent and formidable shout of reprobation, in which only

a few resounding words are, with difficulty, perceived: "Shame! Shame! . . . Stone her! Stone her! . . . Death! Death! . . . Stone her!" etc. All this is accompanied by a noise of flight, of hurrying footsteps, of sticks and pebbles clashing, of broken branches, etc.)

SILANUS.

They have seen her! . . .

VERUS

But what is happening? . . . Is it she whom they are attacking? . . .

SILANUS

It is what I feared. . . . We must take care . . .

VERUS (*rushing to the bottom of the garden*).

This way! . . . Follow me! . . . Appius, Cœlius, your swords! . . .

(*At the moment when he rushes down, the laurel-hedge is burst through in every part by the yelling and gesticulating crowd pursuing* MARY MAGDALENE. *She makes a frenzied attempt to reach the terrace.* VERUS *and his two friends run towards her, to try to protect her against the invading multitude. Stones fly.* VERUS, *standing in front of the others, brandishes his bare sword. Just as the fighting is about to begin, when already branches are broken, a statue overturned and so forth, suddenly a loud call of the supernatural voice rings under the nearer olive-trees. All cease, struck with stupor. A word of command is passed from mouth to mouth: "Silence! Silence! . . . . . Listen! Listen! . . .*

He is speaking! He is going to speak! . . . The Master has made a sign! . . . Listen! Listen! . . ." Then, in the silence thus suddenly produced, the divine voice rises, calm, august, profound and irresistible.)

THE VOICE

He that is without sin among you, let him first cast a stone at her! . . .

(*The stones are heard to drop to the ground. The crowd sways to and fro, abashed, and disappears gradually, in silence, through the hedge.* VERUS *comes forward to support* MARY MAGDALENE, *who has stopped and is standing erect and motionless in the middle of the walk. She rejects the proffered aid, with a harsh and fierce gesture, and, staring in front of her, alone among the others, who look at her without understanding, slowly she climbs the steps of the terrace.)*

CURTAIN

ACT II

ACT II

(*The Tablinum* [*or large room behind the Atrium*] *of* MARY MAGDALENE'S *villa at Bethany. At the back, leading one into the other, the Atrium and a long vestibule with marble columns.*)

SCENE I

MARY MAGDALENE, LUCIUS VERUS

(ENTER LUCIUS VERUS. MARY MAGDALENE *runs up to him and throws herself into his arms.*)

MARY MAGDALENE.

You at last, my Verus! . . . For three days I have awaited you, for three days I have called you. Men grant me my beauty when its triumph brings me nothing but regret and disgust. And I ask myself, is that beauty really powerless when, at last, there is a question of the happiness which every woman has the right to expect in her life? . . .

VERUS

I know not if I shall be able to give you the happiness that is your due, Magdalene; but be assured that your beauty never gained a more complete victory. . . .

MARY MAGDALENE

What care I now for its victory! . . . It is I who am vanquished, utterly vanquished beforehand, without daring to confess it to myself, without being able to hide it from my indifference, so odiously acquired, or from my vanity, which has never been more than the shameful crown of my shame! . . . But why keep me waiting so long? . . . I thought that everything was abandoning me, that all was lost because of the dreadful words which I spoke at our good Silanus' and which were not true, which were only a profounder lie then my other lies, because I was mad, because I did not know, because I did not wish for an impossible happiness. . . .

VERUS

You well know, Magdalene, that I never believed you the woman you depicted. . . . But now neither do I dare believe in the happiness that approaches. . . . I am quite dazzled, I doubt, I grope in the dark. . . . I do not recognize the voice that has so often and so harshly repelled me.

MARY MAGDALENE (*in* VERUS' *arms*)

It is not the same voice, it is not the same soul. . . .

VERUS

And yet it is really you whom I hold in my arms, it is every parcel of you whom I have implored so long! . . . I ask myself still if all is indeed real, if all is indeed possible, if you are not trifling with a too-credulous happiness which you will fling aside among all those which beauty shatters when testing its power. . . . But no, when I question, when I follow your eyes that plunge into mine, I see that it is indeed true, that it was always true. . . .

MARY MAGDALENE

Yes, yes, it is true, it is true and it was always true. . . . I did not know it, I searched my heart in vain and I was ignorant of all my feelings until these days of anguish. . . . I refused to see that you were coming towards me and that everything was awaiting you. . . . And yet I ought to have known it. . . . Already, at Antioch, do you remember, Verus, how I avoided you? . . . I received so many others; and you alone, the comeliest, the purest, I tried to ignore, to blot out, to destroy. . . . As soon as you appeared, I withdrew, like a shy and distrustful animal, to my lair; and, only the other day, at our good Silanus', I felt all the evil, all the cruelty, or all the despair that fills my heart rise to my lips. . . . But, to-day, I see; I am no longer the same; I no longer know myself, because I am myself once more. . . . All that used to resist is broken within my soul. . . . I no longer understand myself and I did not know that happiness is so strange a thing. . . . I, who never wept in my worst moments of distress, am sobbing to-day when happiness awaits me. . . . I am glad and light-hearted and yet more shattered than if all the misfortunes that hover in the skies were about to burst over me. . . . (*Embracing him more passionately*) Help me, my Verus, help me, support me, you whom nothing threatens, you who have nothing to fear! . . .

VERUS

But what has happened? Can any one have dared, in my absence . . . .?

MARY MAGDALENE

No, no, nobody; and it is not that; and I myself do not know the danger that surrounds me. . . . But I have no other shelter than your arms; and I feel myself lost if I lose you too. . . . Take me, bear me away on that heart to which I am listening, far from myself, far from this place and from my anxiety. . . . You alone can save me and I have no life but that which you give me. . . . But why did you forsake me so long in my tears, why did you not come until after the third day, abandoning me thus, without a word of pity, without a sign of hope? . . .

VERUS

You are mistaken, Magdalene, or else your slaves did not acquaint you with the truth. . . . The very day after our meeting at Silanus', I came to Bethany to tell you that, by order of the Procurator, I was suddenly sent, at the head of a cohort, to suppress a curious riot that had broken out near Jericho. The slaves who keep your door would not allow me to approach you and replied to me in such a way that I dared not well insist. . . . I understood that they were obeying orders so precise and so stern that I must not try to thwart them. . . .

MARY MAGDALENE

It is true. . . . I forgot. . . . I was mad and worn out, incapable of seeing, willing or hearing. . . . I was not yet awake. . . . It seemed to me that I was still struggling amid the hideous crowd in Simon's garden, where I called in vain upon him who had delivered me. . . . He was abandoning me, he too. . . . I sent in search of him to no purpose. No one could tell me where he was hiding. . . . Have you not seen him since? . . . Do you not know where he is? . . .

VERUS

Who?

MARY MAGDALENE

The Nazarene. . . .

VERUS

Let us not speak of that wretched man: his hours are numbered. . . .

MARY MAGDALENE

His hours are numbered? . . . What do you mean? . . .

VERUS

No matter: that does not interest us now and soon we shall know nothing of aught that does not touch our love; for it is wonderful to see how the thoughts of those who love each other meet and unite in spite of the distance and of the ill-natured speeches that come between them. Is it not astonishing that, after leaving you at Silanus', where I had heard words that should have deprived me of all hope, I for the first time felt our young happiness swell and blossom in all its strength and all its certainty? . . . While you were calling me, I called you also with all the deep and wonderful voices of my heart. I was kept far from you by a duty unworthy of a soldier; for that expedition to Jericho, the last, I trust, upon which I shall be sent, was almost odious and often ridiculous. I counted with rage the minutes stolen from our new life, which was already beginning in a soul that feared none of my reasons for fearing. . . .

MARY MAGDALENE

It will not really begin until we are far from this land where I suffocate, where everything darkens and threatens happiness, where I can no longer live. . . . Verus, I beseech you, if you love me as I love you, let us hasten, let us leave everything; there is no time to lose. . . .

VERUS

You are right: a joy so long awaited must not be born among these sinister rocks, where floats an odour of death and madness. . . . And yet, even here, our thoughts came to an understanding long before our words. . . . Like you, I have resolved to leave this hated city, where really my obedience is abused. . . . I am at the orders of the Procurator, but not at the venomous service of the Jewish priests, nor of the clamorous and perfidious nation whom my old legionaries have conquered. I have had enough of this ambiguous life. Before to-night, I shall find a pretext for evading an order which I was to execute this very day, an order of which I but too well know the origin. . . . If the pretext appear insufficient, let Caiaphas and Annas go and complain to Cæsar. . . . Nothing counts in the presence of our love; and the inglorious errand which they claim the right to impose upon me repels me all the more inasmuch as it was to be accomplished, so to speak, before your eyes. . . .

MARY MAGDALENE

Before my eyes? . . . Of what are you speaking? . . .

VERUS

Nothing that interests you; let us think only of our happy escape. . . .

MARY MAGDALENE

I know that some danger threatens him. . . .

VERUS

Whom do you mean? . . .

MARY MAGDALENE

It is impossible, after what he has done,

that you should become the instrument of his worst enemies. . . . You owe him my life and perhaps our happiness. . . . What do they want with him? What orders have you received? . . .

VERUS

I am charged to arrest him before this evening, together with the principal leaders of his band. It is a vulgar constabulary measure, directed against sick men and vagrants, of a kind that has never yet been exacted of the legionaries. . . . It shall not take place; do not let us speak of it. . . .

MARY MAGDALENE

But why arrest him? What has he done? What is he accused of? . . . He is innocent, I know; besides, one need but see him to understand. . . . He brings a happiness that was not known before;

and all those who come near him are happy, it seems, like children at their awaking. . . . I myself, who only caught a glimpse of him among the olive-trees, felt that gladness was rising in my soul like a sort of light that overtook my thoughts. . . . He fixed his eyes for but a moment on mine; and that will be enough for the rest of my life. . . . I knew that he recognized me without ever having seen me and I knew that he wished to see me again. . . . He seemed to choose me gravely, absolutely, for ever. . . .

VERUS

What does this mean? Are you speaking of him? What happened? . . . Have you seen him again? . . . I was told, for that matter, that he is an intriguer, ready for everything; but I should never have believed that he would have dared . . .

MARY MAGDALENE

He has dared nothing. . . . I have not seen him again, I shall never see him again, now that we are about to leave everything, to be only we two alone. . . .

VERUS (*clasping her more closely*)

To be one alone, Magdalene, in a happier land, where everything encourages happiness, smiles upon lovers and blesses beauty. . . .

MARY MAGDALENE (*bursting into convulsive sobs on* VERUS' *breast*)

I love you. . . . I know it. . . .

VERUS

Come, I know these tears that well at the same moment from our two hearts in our one joy. . . . But here, between the columns of the vestibule, come the greatest ornaments of that beautiful Rome which we shall soon astonish with our love. . . . I am right: it is our good Silanus, accompanied by the faithful Appius; led by the immortal gods, they descend the marble steps to hallow with their fraternal presence the first smiles of a happiness born under their eyes. . . .

SCENE II

The same, SILANUS, APPIUS

SILANUS

It was said and it was written that, on this most propitious day, I should behold two marvels, not the lesser of which is to see thus promptly reunited two lovers who, according to love's ancient custom, should have fled from each other the more obstinately the more they yearned to meet. . . .

APPIUS

By Metrodorus, Hermachus and Zeno, there are other things on hand than the too-long-expected happiness of two lovers cutting short their quarrels! . . . Tell them at once what has happened; shout it to them, with all your throat and all your soul: death no longer exists! The graves are about to open, the spirits of the dead to show themselves; the gods are shaken, all the laws of life are overturned! . . . We have just admired an unequalled, unspeakable, unheard-of phenomenon, that has never been seen since light first rose upon the world, that will not be seen again before the death of the gods! . . .

SILANUS

The more extraordinary it seems to you, Appius, the less should it trouble the perfect composure of your soul, considering that a phenomenon that will not be seen again could not well shake the laws of the universe nor the stability of the gods!

VERUS

But what has happened? Appius seems to be the victim of a greater exaltation than usual; and you yourself, my worthy master, despite your even mind . . .

APPIUS

I will tell you what has happened: he has brought a dead man to life! . . .

MARY MAGDALENE

Who? . . .

SILANUS

The Nazarene, whose return I have come to announce to you, as I promised.

MARY MAGDALENE

He has come back? Since when? Where is he? . . . Have you seen him? . . .

SILANUS

To reply to your questions in order, lady, I will tell you that he returned this morning, that I saw him with my eyes and that, at this moment, he is with my neighbour Simon the Leper. I am surprised, however, that the absolute frenzy which has shaken the country for two or three hours has not yet spread as far as here. It is true that your dwelling is separated by a high hill and some olive-woods from the spot where the sepulchre lies hidden.

MARY MAGDALENE

I have heard nothing, learned nothing. . . . In spite of my orders, no one has told me. . . . . But, after all, what has happened? . . . Appius is as pale as a ghost. . . . What is it? What has he said, what has he done? . . . .

APPIUS

He has done a thing which no man, no god, has done before him; a thing which I would not have believed if ten thousand witnesses had come to swear it in the name of the immortals, but in which I believe as firmly as I am bound to believe in my own existence, having seen it with my eyes, as I see you now, and almost touched it with my hands, as I touch this vase. He said, "Rise, come forth and walk." And the dead man rose, came forth and began to walk among us!

VERUS

It was apparently a dead man whose health left nothing to be wished for? . . .

SILANUS

No, I am convinced that it was really a dead man.

APPIUS

It was a real, a terrible dead man! . . . If not, my senses can no longer declare that the sun shines in the blue or that human flesh decays! . . . He had been four days in the grave! . . .

MARY MAGDALENE

But who? How? Where? . . . And the Nazarene? . . . I want to know. . . . Speak for him, Silanus: he has not yet recovered his senses. . . .

SILANUS

Here, in a few words, is what happened. Nevertheless, it is right that I should tell you that I do not entirely share Appius' amazement. It should astonish us no more to see a man return to life than to see a child come to life or an old man leave it. (MAGDALENE *makes a movement of impatience.*) But I understand your impatience. I spoke to you the other day of my neighbour Simon. He lives in the little house that touches my property, with his wife, his sister-in-law and his brother-in-law, named Lazarus. This Lazarus, whom I saw only two or three times, for he was often away from home, had been ailing for some weeks and died four days ago. . . .

APPIUS

Four days, do you understand? . . . That is what nobody would dare deny. . . .

SILANUS

Nor does any one think of doing so, Appius. They were a very united family;

and the sorrow of those poor people was great. From my terrace, I could hear the lamentations of the women. According to the custom of the Jews, Lazarus was buried on the night that followed after his death. They laid him in a new grave, dug in the rocks that form the other side of that hill, and closed the grave with an enormous stone. This morning, suddenly, the rumour spread that the Nazarene had returned and that he was going to restore to life the dead man, who was his friend. Appius, who was at my house, persuaded me to go down with him; and we followed the crowd into the valley of the tombs.

MARY MAGDALENE

I knew that he was to return to-day; but why did you not send word to me at once, as you promised? . . .

SILANUS

It seemed to me that the spectacle at hand was not one of those on which the eyes of a woman in the hour of her beauty love to rest. Moreover, there was cause to fear lest your arrival among the excited crowd should cause a repetition of the violence of the other day. For an enormous crowd, silent, but quivering like a swarm of bees, escorted the Nazarene, in front of whom walked the two sisters of Lazarus. We, Appius and I, climbed on to a block of stone hidden behind some bushes, whence we could see and hear everything without arousing the suspicion of the Jews. They showed the grave to the Nazarene, who stopped and lowered his head.

APPIUS

He wept. They whispered in the

crowd, "Behold how he loved him!" But nobody dared approach. They formed a circle at a distance, as though round a dread being. . . .

SILANUS

"Take ye away the stone," said the Nazarene; and two men stepped toward the grave.

APPIUS

You forget that, at that moment, one of the sisters of the dead man, alarmed and all in tears, seized the Nazarene by the arm and said, "Lord, by this time he stinketh; for he hath been dead four days." The Nazarene answered—I have not forgotten a single one of his words—"Said I not unto thee that, if thou wouldest believe, thou shouldest see the glory of God? Take ye away the stone."

MARY MAGDALENE

Who is this sister of Lazarus? Is she Simon's wife?

SILANUS

No, it is the other one: her name is Mary and, when the Nazarene stays at Bethany, she never leaves him.

MARY MAGDALENE

Is she young?

SILANUS

She is younger than Simon's wife.

MARY MAGDALENE

Have you seen her? Do you know her? . . .

SILANUS

I have spoken to her more than once. But to return to the stone, which was enormous, flat and fastened into the walls of the cave: two men attacked it with levers. It resisted at first and then, suddenly, fell down all of a piece. . . .

APPIUS

We were quite close, hanging aslant over the cave. By all the gods who from heaven rule the earth and men, I swear that, at that moment, I felt the terrible breath of the dead man strike me in the face! . . .

MARY MAGDALENE

Did you see the dead man? . . .

APPIUS

As I see you now, lady! . . .

VERUS

I do not understand how you can seriously interest yourselves in these things which happen in an incongruous, mad world, where all is witchcraft, coarse illusions and barbarous lies. . . .

APPIUS

By Hades and Persephone, what my senses perceived was no illusion, I assure you! . . . We nearly fell from our rock! . . . The corpse was there, in the greedy light that devoured the cave, lying like a stiff and shapeless statue, closely bound in grave-clothes, the face covered with a napkin. The crowd, heaped up in a semicircle, irresistibly attracted and repelled, leaned forward, stretched its thousand necks, without daring to approach. The Nazarene stood alone, in front. He raised his hand, spoke a few words which I did not catch and then, addressing the corpse in a voice whose pent-up force I shall never forget, he cried, "Lazarus, come forth!"

MARY MAGDALENE

Did he come forth? . . .

APPIUS

We heard only the sound of the wind moving the garments of the multitude and the buzzing of the flies that swarmed into the grave. All eyes were so firmly fixed upon the corpse that I saw, so to speak, their motionless beams, as one sees the sunbeams in a dark room. . . . Suddenly, it became plain, terrifying, superhuman! The dead man, obeying the order, slowly bent in two; then, snapping the bandages that fastened his legs, he stood up erect, like a stone, all white, with his arms bound and his head veiled. With small, almost impossible steps, guided by the light, he came forth from the grave. The affrighted crowd gradually fell back, without being able to turn away its gaze. "Loose him and let him go," said the Nazarene. And the two sisters of the dead man, releasing themselves from the human hedge, rushed to their brother.

MARY MAGDALENE

And he? . . .

APPIUS

He staggered, he stumbled at every step. . . .

MARY MAGDALENE

But the Nazarene? . . .

APPIUS

He went away without a word and withdrew into Simon's house.

VERUS

And the dead man, how did he go? . . .

APPIUS

The two sisters, wild-eyed, mechanically, blindly fumbled and cut the napkin and the grave-clothes; then, supporting the dead man and helping him to walk, they led him away to the same house. The crowd dared not follow them save with their eyes. No one uttered a word; even the two women did not yet speak to the dead man.

MARY MAGDALENE

And the Nazarene? Has he been seen again?

SILANUS

He has not left Simon's house. The swaying multitude is waiting for him in the orchard and along the roads; for, after the first long minutes of stupor, reaction set in and a general alacrity followed. . . .

APPIUS

Which was as extraordinary as the miracle itself! First, a confused and almost dumb gladness, made up of whispers that seek and feel for one another, passed through the crowd. Then, as though the truth had suddenly burst forth under the skies, an unspeakable gaiety seized upon the mass. The whispers became cries that were not recognizable. The women, the children and especially the older men exulted frantically. It was as though they were trampling on death, which a god had just conquered and laid low, for the first time since man came into existence. At this moment, an inconceivable and dangerous exaltation still prevails in all the region round about the tombs; and, by Hercules, though we have escaped unscathed, I would not advise my worst enemy to risk the Roman toga and arms there!

VERUS

Is that all? . . .

APPIUS

What more would you have? . . .

VERUS

I should like to know what all this proves.

APPIUS

It proves that this man who has conquered death, which hitherto had conquered the world, is greater than we and our gods. It therefore behoves us to hear what he has to tell us and to conform our lives to it.

SILANUS

I will conform mine to it, Appius, if what he teaches is better than what I have learned. By awaking a dead man, in the depth of his grave, he shows us that he possesses a power greater than that of our masters, but not a greater wisdom. Let us await everything with an even mind. It is not difficult, even for a child, to discern that which, in men's words, augments or decreases the love of virtue. If he can convince me that I have acted wrong until to-day, I will amend, for I seek only the truth. But, if all the dead who people these valleys were to rise from their graves to bear witness, in his name, to a truth less high than that which I know, I would not believe them. Whether the dead sleep or wake, I will not give them a thought unless they teach me to make a better use of my life. . . .

MARY MAGDALENE (*starting*)

Listen! . . . .

VERUS

What is it? . . .

APPIUS

I hear stones rolling. . . .

VERUS

It is like the murmur of a crowd. . . .

MARY MAGDALENE

He is coming! . . .

APPIUS (*going to the first columns of the vestibule*)

From here we overlook the wall of the first court. . . . I see them! . . .

MARY MAGDALENE (*pale and staggering, takes a few steps toward the back of the Atrium and gazes into the distance*)

Yes. . . .

APPIUS

They are wrapped in a cloud of dust. . . . There are two or three thousand of them crowding toward the entrance. . . . I think it is those who were at the grave. . . .

VERUS

They would not dare! . . .

MARY MAGDALENE

Verus! . . .

VERUS

Fear nothing, Magdalene: this time, I alone will defend you.

APPIUS

They are following, at a distance, a man clad in white, who is entering the court. . . .

VERUS

But what is the janitor of the first courtyard doing? . . . Will he not stop him? . . .

APPIUS

Yes. . . . He is coming now. . . . What is he doing? . . . One would think he was afraid! . . . He suddenly stops and lets him pass without a word. . . .

VERUS

And the others follow him. . . . They are entering the second court. . . . The impudence of those Jews is really incredible! . . . In Rome, even during the Saturnalia, we should not allow the crowd to push its way like that. . . . What are the slaves doing? . . .

MARY MAGDALENE

Is it he? . . .

SILANUS

Who? . . .

MARY MAGDALENE

The Nazarene. . . .

SILANUS

I think not. . . . It is not his walk. . . . I believe rather that it is . . .

APPIUS

There he is, in the plane-tree avenue!

SILANUS

He is coming straight in our direction. . . .

VERUS

He is even taking the shortest way. He is coming up the steps under the boxwood arbour. . . . He seems at home. . . . Fortunately, the slaves are running from every side to bar his entrance to the vestibule. . . .

MARY MAGDALENE

Hush, I entreat you! . . .

VERUS

What is the matter? . . .

APPIUS

He is coming nearer; he is terribly pale. . . .

SILANUS

I believe it is . . .

MARY MAGDALENE

Who? . . .

SILANUS

The other one. . . . The one whom he brought forth from the . . .

MARY MAGDALENE

Lazarus? . . .

SILANUS

Yes, I recognize him. . . .

VERUS

What does he want with us? . . . Ghosts do not walk like that, in broad daylight. . . . He is horrible! . . .

MARY MAGDALENE

Oh, hush, hush! . . .

SILANUS

Here he is. . . .

SCENE III

THE SAME, LAZARUS. *At the back of the vestibule, the* SLAVES. *Further away, imagined rather than perceived, the crowd of* JEWS.

(*A great silence.* LAZARUS *advances slowly from the back of the vestibule. He looks neither to the right nor to the left. The* SLAVES *of the villa, who have hastened up among the last columns, form a group for a moment as though to block his way. But, at the approach of the man risen from the dead, who seems unaware of their presence, they fall back silently, one after the other.* LAZARUS ENTERS *by the back of the Atrium and stops on the threshold, which is raised by three steps.* MARY

MAGDALENE *moves backwards to one of the columns in the foreground, against which she crushes herself, motionless. But* VERUS, *breaking the silence, with his hand on the hilt of his sword, goes up to* LAZARUS.)

VERUS (*in a hectoring voice*)

Who are you? . . . (LAZARUS *does not reply.*) You do not answer? . . . It is indeed easier to cover with silence what one dare not confess. But, if you have nothing to say, you have no business here. It is well for you that my pity is stronger than my indignation. Go!

(*A new and profound silence.*)

LAZARUS (*in a voice that does not seem yet to have recovered its human note, to* MAGDALENE)

Come. The Master calls you.

(MAGDALENE *leaves the column against which she is leaning and takes four or five steps towards* LAZARUS, *as though walking in her sleep.*)

VERUS (*barring the road*)

Where are you going? . . .

MARY MAGDALENE (*as though recovering consciousness with difficulty, in a stifled, hesitating voice, which she vainly tries to render firmer*)

Wherever he wishes. . . .

VERUS

No, not while I am here! . . .

MARY MAGDALENE (*throwing herself convulsively into* VERUS' *arms*)

Verus! . . .

VERUS (*clasping her violently*)

Have no fear, Magdalene. Nothing can touch you in these arms which close round you. The madness of this land seems more contagious than its pestilence and more tenacious than its leprosy; but Roman reason does not waver, like the rest, at the first foul breath that issues from a tomb. We will cut this matter short. (*To* LAZARUS) You I will not touch with my sword. It shrinks from corpses, even when they walk and drive the trade which you do. It is for the slaves to show you the road back to the sepulchre. . . . Where are the slaves? . . . But, before going, look at this and tell your master that the woman whom he covets—by the gods, he lacks neither taste nor daring!—has sought a refuge in these arms, which will know how to defend her against his barbarous witchcraft and his childish spells. Above all, repeat to him what I am about to say: he will perhaps understand. His life, which will not be a long one, after what he has done, lies wholly in this hand which drives you hence. I have spoken. Go. She will not follow you. . . .

MARY MAGDALENE (*struggling to escape from* VERUS' *embrace, while, in the effort, her hair becomes loosened and falls over her shoulders*)

Yes! . . .

VERUS (*holding her back by force*)

What does this mean? . . . Then you wish to . . .? (MAGDALENE *nods her head.*) I no longer understand. . . . Or rather I begin to understand too well. . . . You were at one. . . . And it was he whom you were awaiting with that impatience which seemed so sweet to me? . . . For who could be made to believe that the fairest, richest and proudest woman in all Judea would thus, without a previous understanding, obey the first word, the first sign of the grotesque and repulsive messenger sent by one whom she had seen but once in her life! . . . It is too much. . . . I see, I know: go, since you love him! . . .

MARY MAGDALENE

No, no! . . . I love you, but he. . . .

VERUS

But he? . . .

MARY MAGDALENE (*sinking in sobs at* VERUS' *feet*)

It is a different thing! . . .

VERUS

It is well, stand up. . . . I do not keep you by force. But I could not have believed that you had come to this. . . . I have fallen into one of your Jewish traps. Do you see the crowd posted there, under the portico, spying upon its hostages? . . . I will not have Roman property defiled. . . . I bear you no grudge, Magdalene. Love, in me, is not extinguished in a moment; and I possess more constancy than woman. . . . I shall watch over you. I know now that, by destroying him, I can save her whom he wished to destroy. He does not suspect that he owes his life to me; for hitherto, from pity or indifference, I had held back the threats that were gathering over his head. But, since he himself comes to attack me in my happiness, I add to those threats all the weight of flouted love. . . . And, now, go with your guide from the tombs. . . . We shall meet again before long.

(LAZARUS GOES OUT *slowly through the vestibule.* MAGDALENE, *without a word, without a movement, without a look,* GOES OUT *after him, amid the profound, still silence of all present.*)

APPIUS (*after a long pause*)

We have this day seen more than one thing that we had not seen before. . . .

SILANUS

It is true, Appius; and this is as surprising as the resurrection of a dead man.. .. . .

CURTAIN

ACT III

ACT III

(*In the house of* JOSEPH OF ARIMATHÆA. *The Supper-room in which the Last Supper took place. Windows at the back. Doors to the right and left. Judæo-Roman architecture. The lamps are lit. It is the end of the night of the sixth of April.*)

SCENE I

NICODEMUS. LEVI THE PUBLICAN. SIMON THE LEPER. LAZARUS, THE MAN RISEN FROM THE DEAD. CLEOPHAS, ZACCHÆUS. THE MAN THAT WAS BORN BLIND. BARTIMÆUS, THE BLIND MAN OF JERICHO. THE MAN OF GERASA POSSESSED BY A DEVIL. THE IMPOTENT MAN OF BETHESDA. THE MAN HEALED OF A DROPSY. THE MAN WHOSE

HAND WAS WITHERED. SIMON PETER'S MOTHER-IN-LAW MARY CLEOPHAS. SALOME, THE WIFE OF ZEBEDEE. SUSANNA. *Several nameless* MEN AND WOMEN CURED BY MIRACLES. *A few* HUNCHBACKED, HALT, BLIND, LEPERS *and* PALSIED *waiting to be healed. Some* BEGGARS, *two or three* HARLOTS, *etc.* (*All these people are struck with consternation and alarm at the arrest of* JESUS *and at the bad news that is current. They crowd at the back of the room, muttering and whispering.* ENTER MARTHA, *the sister of* LAZARUS.)

MARTHA (*affrighted, looking anxiously around her*)

I have seen him!

(*Sensation.* ALL *gather eagerly round* MARTHA.)

NICODEMUS

Where is he? . . .

MARY CLEOPHAS

Has he suffered? . . .

SALOME

What does he say? . . .

MARTHA

Where is my sister? . . .

MARY CLEOPHAS

She is with her mother, in our host's chamber. . . . Her mother was worn out with sorrow. . . .

MARTHA (*going to one of the windows*)

Did no one follow me? . . . No, the street is empty. . . . I went a long way round. . . .

NICODEMUS

Where did you see him? . . .

MARTHA

He was coming out of Annas' palace. . . . I followed him to Caiaphas'. . . . It seems they are looking for us. . . . They have a special grudge against Lazarus, the man raised from the dead. . . . Where is he? . . .

NICODEMUS (*pointing to* LAZARUS, *in the shadow*)

Here, among us. . . .

MARTHA

They mean to arrest all those who went with him. . . . They mean to stone us according to the law. . . . They will persecute all those who come from Galilee. . . .

CLEOPHAS

We are all Galileans. . . . .

A MAN CURED BY A MIRACLE

No, not I. . . .

ANOTHER

Nor I: I am from Bethany.

BARTIMÆUS

And I from Jericho. . . . .

A MAN CURED BY A MIRACLE

It is not well that we should be found together. . . .

NICODEMUS

Where will you go? . . . .

A MAN CURED BY A MIRACLE

No matter where. . . . We shall be safer than here. . . .

ANOTHER

They do not know us. . . . I have never been seen with him. . . .

A WOMAN

Nor I either: he just simply healed me. . . . I was bowed together and he made me straight. . . .

A MAN

I saw him only once: it was when he said to me, "Arise and take up thy bed and go thy way into thine house." I am he whom they let down through the roof upon a bed. . . . Now I walk like other men. . . . (*He turns to the door and* GOES OUT, *followed by* THOSE CURED BY MIRACLES *who spoke before him.*)

A SICK MAN

They are right. . . . We are not

known either. . . . I came to be healed of a dysentery. . . . I have not had time to touch him. (*He also makes for the door.*)

MARTHA

Are you not ashamed? . . .

THE SICK MAN (*stopping on the threshold*)

Of what? . . . It serves no purpose that those whom he has healed should perish because of him. . . . (*He* GOES OUT.)

ANOTHER MAN CURED BY A MIRACLE

He can do nothing for us, because he can do nothing for himself; and we can do nothing for him. . . .

A HUNCHBACK

Yes, why does he not protect us? . . . He is constantly speaking of his father and the angels. . . . Where are those angels?

NICODEMUS

It is because his hour has not yet come.

THE HUNCHBACK

When will his hour come? . . . When it is too late. . . . I have not the time to wait. . . . (*He* GOES OUT.)

NICODEMUS

Let those who do not love him go. . . . The Son of Man shall come in such an hour as you think not. . . .

CLEOPHAS

His kingdom is not of this world. . . .

A BLIND MAN

His kingdom is lost. . . .

NICODEMUS

He said, "Are not five sparrows sold for two farthings and not one of them is forgotten before God?" . . . .

CLEOPHAS

He said, "Live not in careful suspense." . . .

NICODEMUS

He said, "If a man keep my saying, he shall never see death." . . .

THE BLIND MAN

But he also said, "Let the dead bury their dead." (*He gropes his way to the door and* GOES OUT.)

A LAME MAN

I am going away, not that I am afraid, but to go and look for him. . . . .

ANOTHER

I also. . . . (*They* GO OUT.)

A LEPER

Who said that we must wait for him here? . . .

NICODEMUS

Simon Peter.

THE LEPER

Where is Simon Peter? . . . He hardly shows himself.

MARTHA

He was by the fire, in the high-priest's hall. . . .

NICODEMUS

And John? . . .

MARTHA

I heard that he was in Annas' house. . . .

NICODEMUS

And what was the Master doing when you saw him? . . .

MARTHA

I saw him only for a moment, while he passed between the columns of the vestibule. . . . There was a great crowd around him. . . .

MARY CLEOPHAS

Did he see you? . . .

MARTHA

Yes. He looked at me. . . .

NICODEMUS

He was not free? . . .

MARTHA

His hands were bound. . . . The Roman soldiers were striking him to make him walk faster. . . .

MARY SALOME

Oh! . . . .

CLEOPHAS

And the others, the twelve, where are they? . . .

MARTHA

Nobody knows. . . . . They were seized with panic. . . . I have heard that Thomas and Jude have fled to Galilee. . . . .

NICODEMUS

And Mary Magdalene, did you see her? . . .

MARTHA

No, but James met her. . . . She is mad with grief, it seems. . . . She was crying out, tearing her garments and dashing her head against the walls in Annas' palace. . . . The servants drove her away; and, since then, nobody knows what became of her. . . . A poor man told me that she was wandering in the Roman quarter. . . .

NICODEMUS

Does she know that we are here? . . .

MARTHA

Yes, Simon Peter told her. . . .

A SICK MAN

When she comes, do not let her go out again. . . . She will bring misfortune upon us. She is dangerous and does not know what she is doing. . . .

A MAN CURED BY A MIRACLE

There are men marching in the street. . . . I hear the sound of arms. . . . They are coming to arrest us! . . . Let all escape who can! . . . (*To* NICODEMUS, *who is going to a window*) Do not go to the windows, you will be recognized! . . .

BARTIMÆUS

I will go, I am not known, I am from Jericho. . . . (*He looks cautiously into the street*). It is twelve soldiers, with a centurion. . . . Hush! . . . Do not speak! . . .

NICODEMUS

Are they stopping? . . .

BARTIMÆUS

No. . . . They are passing. . . .

There is no one in the street now. . . . Yes! . . . There is some one coming at the other end. . . . Do not make a noise. . . . It is a woman and four men. . . . Why, I know them! . . . It is Mary Magdalene, Joseph of Arimathæa, James, I believe, and Andrew and Simon Zelotes. . . . They are looking around them. . . . They are knocking. . . . Go down and open the door to them. . . .

SCENE II

THE SAME, MARY MAGDALENE, JOSEPH OF ARIMATHÆA, JAMES, ANDREW *and* SIMON ZELOTES

MARY MAGDALENE (*beside herself, dishevelled, barefoot, with torn garments*)

How many are you? . . . Are you

ready? . . . What have you been doing while waiting for me? . . . I have come from the Antonia Tower. . . . The military tribune was not in the Roman quarter. . . . But I have seen his friend Appius. . . . He will send him to us as soon as he returns. . . . Verus said that it might be possible to save him. . . . I do not know how. . . . He will explain it to us. . . . But, if he does not save him, we must. . . . James and Simon have swords under their cloaks. Where is Peter? Where is John? . . .

MARTHA

I saw them in the hall of the high-priest's house. . . .

MARY MAGDALENE

They ought to be here. . . . We must be many. . . . He is to pass through this street, under that window, on his way to Pilate. . . .

NICODEMUS

When? . . .

MARY MAGDALENE

To-night, before the second watch. . . . Which of you has arms? Where are they hidden? . . .

NICODEMUS

What do you wish to do? . . .

MARY MAGDALENE

To deliver him, if Verus does not deliver him. . . . It is easy, you shall see. . . . They will let us do as we please, I know they will. . . . The Romans do not want to judge him. . . . Appius told me so, they are perplexed. . . . When they took him to Caiaphas, there were only two soldiers to guard him and two sergeants from the Temple, armed with sticks. . . . If only there had been five or six men with me! . . . We would have hidden him, I know where; and he would have been saved! . . . But I was all alone! . . .

JOSEPH OF ARIMATHÆA

It is not so easy as you think, Magdalene. . . . All the populace was there, ready to stone him. . . .

MARY MAGDALENE

But the populace is on his side and the crowd adores him! . . . You have forgotten his triumphal entry! . . .

JOSEPH OF ARIMATHÆA

It is different now. . . . They were all shouting for his death outside Caiaphas' palace. . . .

MARY MAGDALENE

It was a few servants of the Pharisees and Sadducees. . . .

JOSEPH OF ARIMATHÆA

A few servants would not have been enough to cover a public place to the very roofs. . . . It was indeed the same crowd as on the day of the triumph. . . . No, believe me, Magdalene, he knows what he wishes. . . . He is determined to be destroyed. . . . He has confessed everything. . . .

MARY MAGDALENE

What can he have confessed, when he has done no wrong? . . .

JOSEPH OF ARIMATHÆA

He admitted that he was the Son of God and the King of the Jews.

MARY MAGDALENE

Is it not the truth? . . . .

JOSEPH OF ARIMATHÆA

No doubt, but it would have been better not to proclaim it to-night. In the eyes of the priests and Romans, it is a crime punishable by law. . . .

AN INFIRM MAN

He must be guilty, or they would not have arrested him. . . .

NICODEMUS

We cannot do more than he wishes and commands; and he renounces his defence.

MARY MAGDALENE

But you do not see that he does that to try your faith, your strength, your love! . . . .

NICODEMUS

He foretold all this many times. . . .

MARY MAGDALENE

That was because he knew the cowardice of those who pretended to love him! . . . Ah, men are great and heroic and proud! . . . The only men who have not fled, those who tremble least, the best of you discuss and argue as though they had to do with a measure of wheat; and the women are silent and weep! . . . Well, what do you say, my sisters? . . . Is not this the moment to show your love? . . . And those whom he has healed, where are they, what are they doing? . . . You there, who want to flee, blind Bartimæus, the other one from Jericho, the other from Siloam: those eyes, which he has opened, you turn from me, because I have the courage to speak to you of him!

. . . You, Simon the Leper, you, the other from Samaria, have you forgotten that, before he came, you were more hideous than death? . . . I see nothing around me but miracles in hiding! . . . The man whose hand was withered, the man who was healed of a dropsy on the Sabbath and the man of Gerasa possessed by a devil, who dares not lift up his head! . . . And, among the palsied, he of Bethesda who is running to the door, using his legs only to forsake the God who healed him! . . . Even those whom he raised from the dead are afraid! . . . Why, look at Lazarus: he is more pale than any of you! . . . And yet you saw death, you; you lay touching it for four long days. . . . Is it more terrible than men thought? . . . You do not answer? . . .

(*A long pause.*)

JOSEPH OF ARIMATHÆA

Listen, Magdalene. . . . I lack neither courage nor loyalty. . . . Notwithstanding the power of the priests, I have thrown open my house to those who followed him. I know the price which I shall have to pay. . . . I am prepared to sacrifice everything and life itself to him. But I know his will and I cannot disobey him. . . . Peter wished to defend him and drew his sword. . . . He made him put it up into the sheath. . . . I was at Gethsemane. . . .

MARY MAGDALENE

Since you were there, why did you not help Peter? . . . We save those whom we love; we listen to them afterwards! . . . But what will you do when you have destroyed him? . . . Oh, I am delaying too long with those who are afraid! . . . . What am I doing here, among men who will do nothing? . . I am wasting his last chances and his last minutes. . . . I will go to meet Verus; after him, we shall see. . . . (*She turns to the door.* JOSEPH OF ARIMATHÆA *and* NICODEMUS *block her way.*)

NICODEMUS

Do not go out, Magdalene: it means destroying him and destroying us with him. . . .

MARY MAGDALENE

Ah, destroying you with him, that is the trouble! . . . Wait! (*She takes another step towards the door.* NICODEMUS *stops her resolutely.*)

NICODEMUS

You shall not go out.

MARY MAGDALENE

I shall not go out? . . . True, you dare fight against a woman. I had not foreseen this great courage born of terror. You all shake your heads like empty cornspikes; and the women rejoice in at last discovering the cowardice of the men, showing itself suddenly more signal than their own! . . .

JOSEPH OF ARIMATHÆA

Take counsel, Magdalene; think of him and reflect that, if he heard you . . .

MARY MAGDALENE

Well, if he heard me, it would be as on the day when that one among you whom you all resemble reproached me with anointing his feet with too costly an ointment! . . . Have you forgotten what he said? . . . Whom did he declare to be right? . . . You have understood nothing! . . . For months and years, you have lived in his light; and not one of you has the least idea of what I saw because I loved him, I who did not come until the eleventh hour, I whom he drew from lower than the lowest slave of the lowest among you all! . . .

NICODEMUS (*listening to the sounds outside*)

Hush! . . . Listen! . . . Some one is walking outside the house. . . . (*To* BARTIMÆUS.) Go see who it is. . . .

BARTIMÆUS (*at the window*)

It is a man wrapped in a cloak. . . . A Roman. . . . He has stopped. . . . He knocks at the door. . . . He is coming in. . . . The door was not closed. . . .

MARY MAGDALENE (*running to the door of the Supper-room*).

It is he, it is Lucius Verus! . . . Open the door to him! Open quickly! . . . I hear him! . . .

(*They open the door of the Supper-room.* LUCIUS VERUS *appears in the embrasure. At the sight of the strange assembly of* PERSONS CURED BY MIRACLES, CRIPPLES, BEGGARS *and* SICK, *he stops and stands dumbfounded on the threshold.*)

SCENE III

THE SAME, LUCIUS VERUS

MARY MAGDALENE (*running to* VERUS *with outstretched arms*)

It is you, my Verus, it is indeed you! . . . An eye that looks me in the face, a sword, shoulders, hands that do not tremble! . . . Come! Come! What are we to do? . . . Have you seen him? . . . Where are we going? . . . How can we help him? . . . How many men do you need? . . . Where are yours? He is not only innocent, as you well know, he is so pure, he stands so high that the thoughts of men cannot reach him . . . In his goodness he is bearing everything for the sins of the world; but we will not have him sacrifice himself for us. . . . A single glance from his eyes, a single word from his mouth, are worth all the lives of all other men. . . .

VERUS (*icily*)

Is this indeed the place where I was to meet you? . . . Who are these . . . these men. . . . surrounding you? . . .

MARY MAGDALENE

They can be trusted. . . . They love him as well as he loved them; but they want a leader. . . . They were waiting for you. . . . They will follow you everywhere. . . .

VERUS (*ironically*)

I have not come to command this . . . foreign . . . troop. . . . I do not know what you mean. There is some misunderstanding; and we should not, I think, explain it here, before so many witnesses. . . .

MARY MAGDALENE

You are right. . . . (*To the others*) Leave us. . . . I will call you when the time comes for action. . . .

(ALL GO OUT, *except* MARY MAGDALENE *and* LUCIUS VERUS.)

SCENE IV

LUCIUS VERUS, MARY MAGDALENE

VERUS (*sarcastically*)

Who are those extraordinary persons? . . . I have never seen so many cripples, vagrants and evil-smelling sick people gathered together. . . . What do they want with you? . . . I was told that you were living in the midst of uncouth creatures, the oldest, the ugliest, the dirtiest and the most pestilential of those Jews whom you mocked so pleasantly in the house of the wise Silanus; but I could not have believed that they were so intimate with you as this. . . . However, that no longer concerns me. But I told you that we should meet again before long. . . . Appius informed me that you had been looking for me in the Roman quarter. I left everything to hasten at your first summons. I knew what was happening and I was biding my time. . . .

MARY MAGDALENE

How good and generous you are! . . . How reassuring and comforting your presence and your smile! . . . Those others . . . if you only knew! . . . They were trembling like the reeds of which our Master speaks; and I was helpless and dying with shame. . . . But I knew that you would come back to us; and now this is you, your arms, your breast. . . . It seems to me that Rome in her entirety is protecting us and that your arms, which can do all things, cannot abandon him. . . .

VERUS

They will not abandon you, Magdalene. The rest depends upon yourself alone. . . . I am good and generous, perhaps, but in my own manner; and we must understand each other. . . . So they have arrested him in whom you take so lively an interest, as I told you that they would? . . .

MARY MAGDALENE

They have not only arrested him: all the menials of the Temple, the grooms, the herds, the meanest scullions in the kitchens rushed at him, insulted, flouted and ill-treated him. . . . And, as they were afraid, as they were too cowardly to venture it alone, they made the Roman soldiers help them! . . .

VERUS

I know. . . . But had we not best be brief and to the point? . . .

MARY MAGDALENE

Yes, we have no time to lose. . . .

VERUS

Even so. It is not now a question of arrest nor of more or less justifiable ill-usage, but of imminent death. I have seen the Procurator Pontius Pilate.

MARY MAGDALENE

Good. What did he say? . . .

VERUS

I found him anxious, perplexed, at a loss. He is a mild, irresolute man, an enemy to quarrels and violence. He had to choose between the inevitably bloody revolt of the priests and their sectaries and the sacrifice of an agitator who was unquestionably troublesome and dangerous, but who has not, perhaps, incurred the death penalty in the eyes of Roman law and justice. I spoke according to my duty and conscience. He did not hesitate. He chose the more humane and wiser course. And, as I am the armed guardian responsible for the Roman peace, he gave the fate of your Nazarene into my hands. However, I must admit that, before our interview, I had purposely allowed events to take the course they did. . . .

MARY MAGDALENE

He is saved! I was sure of it! And how right I was to fear nothing and to hope all things in turning to you! . . .

VERUS

Do not let us go too fast. There are many things to consider. . . .

MARY MAGDALENE

What do you say? . . .

VERUS

I say that there are many things to consider. . . . Had I known nothing whatever of your adventure, my choice would not have been in doubt: I should, while more or less pitying him, have sacrificed the wretched man to the public tranquillity; it is the sovereign law of the empire; but now . . .

MARY MAGDALENE

But now, it is different, you know him, you know everything. . . . There is no excuse for a moment's hesitation; it would be monstrous. . . .

VERUS

Indeed, there is no excuse for a moment's hesitation; it would be monstrous, as you say. . . . Shall I, to snatch a favoured rival from a well-merited death, for the second time lose the only woman whom I love or can love? . . . That certainly is impossible. . . .

MARY MAGDALENE

I do not quite understand. . . .

VERUS

Yet it is simple enough: in saving him, I hand you over, without defence, to the fellow who will drag you with him, by fall after fall, to the bottom of none can tell what pit of folly and wretchedness, whence no human and reasoning power will be able to extricate you. Moreover, speaking for myself, I lose you irrevocably by thus giving you, with my own simple, foolish hands, to one who robs me of my happiness by methods against which a man who values the name does not try to struggle. Whereas, if I abandon him to his fate, there remains a chance of seeing you return to the light and for me some prospect of finding you in my path; for our two lives have still, I hope, a long space to cover; and many roads, as you well know, lead to Rome. . . .

MARY MAGDALENE

I understand. . . . I understand, since I needs must understand. . . . But I do not yet believe. . . . No, it is not possible; and you, the man whom I know, have not come to tell me coldly that you wish to destroy him and thus revenge yourself for an injury which he has not done you. . . . There is, there must be, something else. . . .

VERUS

Yes, there is something else. . . . There remains to us, if you are absolutely bent upon it, one means of saving him. But, at the point to which we have come and to which I have driven the adventure, saving him probably means ruin to myself. Besides, time presses. The sentence is written, I have seen it. He will be put to death at daybreak; for the hours are numbered because of the Passover. . . .

MARY MAGDALENE

What must I do? . . . Quick, quick, I will do it. . . .

VERUS

The prisoner is guarded by my men; it is therefore not quite impossible to effect his escape. . . .

MARY MAGDALENE

Why yes, why yes, it is simple; and that, of course, is what we must do! . . . Once free, he will hide and he will be forgotten. . . . Let us lose no time. . . . But I do not understand why you came to say . . .

VERUS

You will soon understand. . . . I answer for the prisoner, therefore. Do you know what I am doing, do you know what I risk by restoring him to liberty? . . .

MARY MAGDALENE

You are only doing your duty in freeing an innocent man. . . .

VERUS

It is not for me to enquire into his innocence; that does not concern me. I am not his judge, but his keeper. . . .

MARY MAGDALENE

Your soldiers will hold their tongues and no one will know that. . . .

VERUS

My soldiers will not be able to hold their tongues. They will have to choose between silence and their lives. It will therefore be known that they acted only on my orders. Now there is no instance of the high-priests' ever abandoning a prey, a revenge, a hatred. They will go and complain, first, at Antioch, to the Governor of Syria, and, next, to Cæsar himself, whose anger is kindled at the very breath of a suspicion. Do you know what Cæsar is? The greatest, the most powerful men in Rome tremble before his shadow. . . . For me, it means, if not death, at least exile far from Rome; and death, to us Romans, seems sweet compared with exile. . . . That is what I give; that is my stake; I am waiting for yours.

MARY MAGDALENE

You are waiting for mine? . . . What would you have me give? . . . I have nothing left. . . . I distributed all to the poor the other evening. . . .

VERUS

I do not ask for what one gives to the poor. . . . And, besides, I have had enough of those evasions which lead to nothing and of those shuffling phrases. . . . Ah, much I care for justice and a vagrant more or less in the world and my own fate and my own exile! . . . Have you not understood that it is you I want, you alone and all of you; that I have wanted you for years; and that this is my hour? . . . It is not beautiful, I know, and it is not as I dreamt it! . . . But it is all I have; and a man takes what he can to make his life! . . . We stand here face to face, with our two madnesses, which are more powerful than ourselves and cannot recede; we must come to an understanding! . . . The more you love him, the more I love you, the more you wish to save him and the more I wish to destroy him! We must come to an understanding! . . . You want his life, I want mine; and you shall have his life, but I shall have you, before he escapes his death. . . . Is it understood? . . . Are we agreed? . . . Say no, if you dare, and let his blood be upon her who has brought him to this pass and who is destroying him twice over! . . .

MARY MAGDALENE

Ah, so that was it! . . . Yes, yes, I know, I see . . . I was not conscious and I no longer thought of it; but it was bound to be. . . . Ah, so it was that which caused me just now, while you were speaking, to have no confidence despite my confidence! . . . It is so strange, so monstrous, so remote from us! . . . One needs a little time to understand. . . .

All one's thoughts become deranged and one's soul falls, falls, like a stone in a well. . . . One grasps the meaning of nothing. . . . One no longer knows where one stands. . . .

VERUS

You and I know quite well; and there is nothing extraordinary in all this. . . . A few days ago, you would not have needed so much urging; and I do not understand that to-day, when the price of love is something quite different, to-day, when a life, dear to you among all lives. . . .

MARY MAGDALENE

Ah, you do not understand! . . . And to think that scarcely any one, not even those who loved him, would understand better! . . . Am I then the only being that has seen into his soul? . . . And yet it is not so very difficult! . . . He has spoken to me only three times in my life, but I know what he thinks. I know all that he wishes, I know all that he is as completely as though I were within him, or as though he were there, near me, fixing upon my brow his glance in which the angels come down from heaven, as on the evening when I kissed his feet and wiped them with my hair. . . .

VERUS

I well knew that I came too late, but I should never have believed that you had gone so far. . . . If he has spoken to you only three times, he has not wasted the minutes and has told you enough to remove my doubts. . . . But let us be calm. It is a question other than of love; and your lover himself, were he consulted, would judge that a kiss does not weigh much in the presence of death. . . . Since you love him so well, is his life not worth a slight displeasure, which but lately would not have inspired you with such horror? . . . If there were a looking-glass in this room, I would go and gaze at myself with curiosity, to make out what, in a few days, has made me so repulsive that the torture of the one man whom you adore is preferred to the touch of my lips! . . . But what is the matter? . . . One would think that I was speaking of unimaginable things! . . . What have I said? What have I done? . . . Your face is distorted. . . . There is no need to look at me like that, with mad and terrified eyes, as though they beheld the fall of the sun or the violation of a tomb! . . .

MARY MAGDALENE

Let me be. . . . You cannot know. . . . I am only beginning to understand. . . .

VERUS

A few days since, you were not so slow in understanding. . . .

MARY MAGDALENE (*in a soft and distant voice*)

Yes, yes. . . . For one sees only little by little. . . . (*Staring before her*) It is unfolded slowly, like a thing that has no beginning, no end, no name. . . . There are two deaths here, I hold two deaths in my hand; and that is too heavy a weight for a poor creature born upon this earth. . . .

VERUS

Two deaths? . . . What do you mean? . . . You do not intend to follow him, surely? . . . Your death, since he loves you, would only add a very useless bitterness to his. . . .

MARY MAGDALENE (*in the same soft and distant voice*)

No. . . . I am not speaking of mine. . . . It is two other deaths. . . . I still have my senses. . . . I can see clearly in the abyss. . . . Let me look, where you can see nothing. . . .

VERUS

I should not have thought that, when I came to bring you his safety and the great sacrifice which I am making to love. . . .

MARY MAGDALENE (*with a sudden outburst*)

The sacrifice which you are making to love! . . . Ah, if you could see the sacrifice which is being accomplished here and which the very angels dare not look upon! . . . But you cannot know what has happened on earth since he descended upon it! . . . It is no longer the same earth; and it is no longer possible! . . . Before he came, the purest would not have hesitated! . . . Before he came! Before he came! . . . And, even then, to-day, I, who have been born again through him, if it were not he, if it were a question of another, I should not have the strength! . . . I should perhaps sin against all that he loves, to save what I love! . . . But he gives too much strength to love and to suffer! . . . I could save him in spite of himself; but no longer in spite of myself! . . . If I bought his life at the price which you offer, all that he wished, all that he loved would be dead! . . . I cannot plunge the flame into the mire to save the lamp! I cannot give him the only death that could touch him! . . . But look at me with clearer eyes and you shall perhaps see all that I perceive without being able to tell you! . . . Were I to yield but for a moment under the weight of love, all that he has said, all that he has done, all that he has given would sink back into the darkness, the earth would be more deserted than if he had not been born and heaven would be closed to mankind for ever! . . . I should be destroying him altogether, destroying more than himself, to gain for him days which would destroy everything. . . .

VERUS

It is not so much a question of gaining days for him as of sparing him tortures, the mere thought of which should make you reflect. . . .

MARY MAGDALENE

I know! I know! . . . Because I love

him thus, as none has ever loved upon this earth where heaven had not yet poured forth its love, must I not sacrifice to him what no human soul has possessed before me? . . . But you come to ask for all that he has given; and what he has given is much more than his life and lives more in our hearts than it lives in himself! . . . If I destroy him in myself, I destroy him in us! . . . I know no more, I see no more, I understand no more. . . . I would do it, perhaps, if my soul were alone; but it is no longer possible and God would not have it! . . .

VERUS

The gods always will what men will. . . . Be sure that, if he whom you are about to deliver to the torture could make his voice heard at this moment, he would not hesitate. . . .

MARY MAGDALENE

Ah, I know that he would not hesitate! And that is why I am struggling thus, like a blind beast, between two sacrifices! . . . It is my past shame that overwhelms me and prevents me from rising to the level of his will! . . . .

VERUS

Man has but one will in the presence of death. . . .

MARY MAGDALENE

My God! My God! . . . I am nothing, I am defiled with every defilement: what matters this one, which brings thee life? . . . But am I in question? . . . Is it not thou alone whom I defile to-day in defiling thy salvation, thou, the very source whence the source of all purity and of every happiness and of every life will spring? . . . I no longer know where to thrust back my soul! . . . Nothing remains to me, if I lose it; nothing remains to us, if I save it! . . .

VERUS

Nothing is lost so long as life endures. . . .

MARY MAGDALENE

Hush, I beseech you! . . . Leave me alone in his silence and his will. . . . Let me contemplate, let me listen to other things. . . . I do not yet love him as he would be loved! . . . In vain I raise my eyes to his heaven of light: I see only his death, his sorrows, his suffering. . . . his steadfast face, his eyes that lit up all he looked upon, his mouth that spoke unceasingly of happiness. . . . his feet which I have kissed, lifeless and icy cold! . . . Verus, Verus, have pity! . . .

I cannot bear it, I cannot bear it! I am falling! . . . Do with me what you will! . . .

VERUS (*catching her in his arms*)

Magdalene, Magdalene! . . . I knew. . . .

MARY MAGDALENE (*springing back at his touch*)

No, you did not know! And it is not that! . . . There is something else! . . . There is another outlet! . . . Verus, Verus, come, you are not without feeling, you are not a monster, you will understand also. . . . It depends on you. . . . For me it is impossible. . . . There is a wall there defended by his angels. . . . I cannot pass it. . . . I must not think of it. . . . But you, you can do everything! . . . To think that you hold there, in that human hand of yours, the life of the

God of Gods descended upon earth! . . . I know, I know, you do not believe it. . . . But you must at least believe in his innocence; and you know that he has done no evil. . . . He does not even know what evil is, since he is all goodness. . . . He has done nothing but heal, console and pray. . . . He has done nothing but breathe over men's souls and flood them with happiness. . . . If only you knew him, if he had spoken to you, were it but once! . . . Because he is innocent and because you are just, because you have strength and because you are brave, you cannot deliver him defenceless to the executioners. . . . It would not be Roman, it would not even be manly. . . .

VERUS

Enough of this; and, as everything is useless, let him be treated as you have decided. . . . It is not I who am leading him to the torture. . . .

MARY MAGDALENE (*clinging to the garments of* VERUS, *who takes a step to the door*)

Verus! Verus! . . . I implore you! . . . That is not all! . . . All is not said! . . . It cannot be decided like this! . . . But do not ask the one impossible thing. . . . I will be your slave, I will live at your feet, serve you on my knees for the rest of my days; but give me his life without destroying in my soul and throughout the earth that which is the very life of our new life! . . .

VERUS

Enough! . . . Besides, there is no time. My patience in saving a rival whom I hate is as ridiculous as your persistent attempt to save your lover by singing his praises! . . . When you see him dead, in less than three hours hence, do not weep over him, lest your tears should be flung back in your own face! . . . (*Perceiving* JOSEPH OF ARIMATHÆA, *who discreetly opens the door, to the left, of the Supper-room.*) Who goes there? . . . Come in, come in, this is the very thing! . . . We need witnesses. Where are the mountebanks, the monsters, the lepers? I want to tell them . . .

MARY MAGDALENE

What? . . .

VERUS

They shall know who has betrayed their god! . . . We shall then see if you have the heart to despatch him before their eyes and how they will take the news! . . . Repugnant though they be, I want to see their ugly faces again! . . . (*He reaches the door and throws it open wide.*)

MARY MAGDALENE (*hurrying to stop his action*)

Verus! Verus! . . . This is not worthy of you! . . .

VERUS

I know! I know! . . . I am not worthy of anything, it appears! Not even of you, harlot! . . . (*Calling in a loud voice*) Hi! Hi! The rest of you! . . . Where are you? . . . Hasten this way, you halt and lame, you club-feet, you cripples, you beggars, vagrants, lepers, paralytics! . . . I have something of importance to tell you! . . . (*Startled faces appear in the embrasures of the two doors.*)

SCENE V

VERUS, MARY MAGDALENE *and nearly* ALL THE CHARACTERS *of* SCENE III

VERUS

Come in, come in, you have nothing to fear! . . . (*They* ENTER, *timidly.*) Are you all there? . . . There seem to be fewer of you. . . . Where are the others gone? . . .

JOSEPH OF ARIMATHÆA

Sir, some of them fear lest the night . . .

VERUS

I understand; they were afraid. . . . Their love and their faith do not take any risk of blows. . . . However, these will do. . . . Do you see that woman? . . . I came to offer to save your master. She had only to say yes. She has said no. She orders his death. He will therefore die at sunrise.

(*Sensation in the crowd.*)

NICODEMUS

What is he saying, Magdalene? . . .

(MARY MAGDALENE *does not reply.*)

VERUS

Ask her, you will learn. . . .

NICODEMUS

Magdalene, is it true? . . .

(MARY MAGDALENE *remains silent.*)

JOSEPH OF ARIMATHÆA

But come, answer! . . . What is the matter with you? . . .

VERUS

She is at the same time betraying and destroying all those who followed the tempter. I have spoken. Farewell. Look to yourselves. (*He turns to the door.*)

JOSEPH OF ARIMATHÆA (*stopping him and beseeching him*)

Sir, I beg of you, do not go away like this. . . . She is mistaken, you will see. . . . There is some terrible misunderstanding. . . . Magdalene, come, what is he saying, what do you say? . . . Why, it is impossible! . . . What has happened? . . .

SEVERAL SICK MEN *and* BEGGARS (*surrounding* MAGDALENE, *who remains motionless, gazing blindly into the distance*)

Magdalene! Magdalene . . . .

A HUNCHBACK

She also has sold him! . . . She was with the Iscariot! . . .

MARTHA (*putting her arms around* MAGDALENE'S *neck*)

Magdalene! . . . Listen to me! . . . You used to love me. . . . What has come to you? . . . Tell me it is not true. . . . You have not heard. . . .

MARY CLEOPHAS (*putting her hand on* MAGDALENE'S *shoulder*)

Magdalene, Magdalene! . . . No, it is impossible. . . . You cannot have forgotten. . . .

A POOR MAN

How much did you receive? . . .

A MAN CURED BY A MIRACLE

Yes, how much? . . . Where is the money? . . .

ANOTHER

Give back the gold! Give back the gold! . . . Search her! . . .

MARY SALOME

Magdalene! Magdalene! . . . She is mad! . . .

A VAGRANT

Harlot! . . . Soldiers' wench! . . .

ANOTHER.

Strumpet! Strumpet! Strumpet!

A MAN CURED BY A MIRACLE

The seven devils whom he cast out have entered her body again! . . .

ANOTHER

She has sold us like a herd of oxen! . . .

A SICK MAN

We shall all have to suffer! . . .

ANOTHER

Yes, but not before she does! . . .

THE MAN WHOSE HAND WAS WITHERED

She shall not go from here until . . .

A PALSIED MAN

In any case, she shall not go hence alive, take my word for it! . . .

(*Almost* ALL, *shouting, gesticulating, threatening, with clenched fists, crowd round* MAGDALENE, *who remains motionless and dumb.*)

JOSEPH OF ARIMATHÆA (*intervening*)

Come, come, do not forget who you are, where you are nor in whose name you are speaking. (*To* VERUS) Sir, I beg of you, a little patience. . . . . I am a just and reasonable man; and everything will be explained. . . . Listen, Magdalene,

I am speaking to you in his name. . . . There is still time to say yes. . . . I am speaking as a father. . . .

(MAGDALENE *maintains her motionless silence.*)

THE HUNCHBACK

You see! . . . She has received the price! . . .

(*An explosion of hatred.* ALL *surround her more closely. The cries, the threats, the imprecations, the entreaties, the moans are redoubled. Suddenly, in the street, rises a tumult which drowns that in the Supper-room. It is the shouting of an angry crowd approaching swiftly, the sound of arms and horses. The uproar in the room is at once lulled.* ALL *listen, anxiously.*)

A MAN CURED BY A MIRACLE

The Romans! . . . The soldiers! . . . They are coming to arrest us! . . . She has betrayed us! . . . Let us fly! . . . This way, this way! . . .

(ALL *lose their heads. Some run wildly round the room, seeking for an outlet.*)

A VAGRANT

No, no! . . . Do not go out! . . . There is only one door! . . . We cannot escape! . . . They would discover us! . . .

A MAN CURED BY A MIRACLE

Be silent! . . . Hide yourselves! . . .

A CRIPPLE

Why do you not put out the lamps?

. . . They will see the lights! . . . Quick! Quick! Put out the lamps! . . .

(*The lamps are put out.*)

ANOTHER

Do not go to the windows! . . . Do not show yourselves at the windows! . . . Lie down along the walls! . . .

VERUS

It is a noble spectacle and I long to see it out. . . .

JOSEPH OF ARIMATHÆA (*going up to* VERUS)

Sir, do not ruin them. . . . They are weak and poor. . . . Almost all of them are sick. . . . They know not what they do. . . . Have pity on men and do not judge them. . . .

(*The shouts—"Crucify him! Crucify him! . . . Tempter! Temp-*

ter! . . . Galilean! Nazarene! . . . He would destroy the Temple! . . . He would destroy the Law! . . . Blasphemer! . . . Crucify him! Crucify him! Crucify him!"—are redoubled in the street and are now heard outside the house itself. The red light of the torches is cast into the room. THE BLIND MAN OF JERICHO *steals up to one of the windows and looks out.*)

A PANIC-STRICKEN VOICE

Do not go to the windows! . . .

A LAME MAN (*going to another window*)

What is happening? . . .

THE BLIND MAN OF JERICHO

It is he! . . .

(*Several* PERSONS, *irresistibly attracted, climb up to the windows and look into the street, with infinite caution. Occasionally* ONE *of them turns to those who remain at the back of the room, to tell them what he sees.*)

ONE OF THOSE AT THE WINDOWS

There are soldiers all around him! . . . . There is a crowd of them! . . .

ANOTHER

He is coming! He is coming this way! . . . His hands are bound! . . . . They are striking him! . . .

ANOTHER

He is weeping! . . . . His eyes are bleeding! . . . .

ANOTHER

They are taking him to Pilate! . . . .

There are Peter and John, hiding themselves! . . . . . .

ANOTHER

The blood is dripping on his feet! . . .

ANOTHER

He cannot walk any farther! . . . He staggers! He staggers! . . . . .

VERUS (*to* MAGDALENE, *who has not moved and who stands against a column, in the middle of the room, staring before her, without turning towards the windows*)

Magdalene! . . . . . .

(*In the street, suddenly, the tumult falls, as a huge, heavy object might fall. A wonderful silence.*)

A VOICE (*in the room*)

What is it? . . . . . .

THE BLIND MAN OF JERICHO (*at the window*)

He falls! . . . He has fallen! . . . He is looking at the house! . . .

VERUS

Magdalene, I still promise you. . . .

MARY MAGDALENE (*without stirring, without looking at* VERUS, *without anger, simply, in a voice from another life, full of peace, full of divine clarity and certainty*)

Go! . . .

THE BLIND MAN OF JERICHO (*at the window*)

He rises to his feet! . . . They drag him along! . . .

(*The tumult, the shouts of "Crucify him!" are resumed and redoubled in the street.* VERUS GOES OUT *slowly, with his eyes on* MAGDALENE, *who remains motionless, as though in ecstasy and all illumined with the light of the departing torches.*)

CURTAIN